An Introduction to
the Life and Works of
JOHN BUNYAN

David Marshall

BISHOPSGATE PRESS

© 1989 David Marshall

British Library Cataloguing in Publication Data
Marshall, D.N. (Derek Norman), *1946-*
John Bunyan.
1. Fiction in English. Bunyan, John, 1628-1688
I. Title
823' .4

ISBN 1-85219-075-2

All enquiries and requests relevant to this title should be sent to the publisher, Bishopsgate Press Ltd., 37 Union Street, London SE1 1SE

Printed by Whitstable Litho Printers Ltd., Millstrood Road, Whitstable, Kent.

CONTENTS

Introduction to the Life and Works of John Bunyan

'We are not afraid to say, that though there were many clever men in England during the latter half of the seventeenth century, there were only two great creative minds. One of those produced the *Paradise Lost*, and the other *The Pilgrim's Progress.'*

Lord Macaulay's equation of the genius of John Bunyan with that of John Milton was considered far-fetched at the time he made it. By the great literary figures among Bunyan's contemporaries it would have been considered outrageous.

To nineteenth-century Bunyan readers his life was encrusted with myth. The tart dismissives of the many enemies of Bunyan in his own lifetime, and his own puritan propensity for self-disparagement, meant that the myth had begun to form before his death. Part of the myth was that of 'the unlettered tinker from Elstow'.

That elements of Bunyan mythology have survived in twentieth-century biographies of the great Nonconformist writer and preacher arises from:-

• The fact that Bunyan continues to be a victim of his own popularity; most of his biographers are ignorant to a surprising degree of seventeenth-century social and political history.

• The fact that the colourful, but largely fictitious, Bunyan of Sir Walter Scott — the gypsy tinker who trudged the villages of Bedfordshire mending kettles

— is more appealing as an evangelical idol than Bunyan himself.

• The tendency to accept *Grace Abounding* (published in 1666) as an autobiography, instead of what is is: an account of an intense search for freedom from guilt and for the assurance of salvation in Christ written in the humble tones of the peniten (but containing next to nothing about his education, civil war military experience, two marriages and his large family).

• The ignorance of more recent biographers and literary commentators of the Puritan Mind, of New Testament theology, and Old Testament history, a knowledge indispensable if one sets out to acquire any more than a superficial view of the man and his work.

John Bunyan was not a tinker of gypsy extraction. Bunyan's allusion in *Grace Abounding*, 'my father's house being of that rank that is meanest and most despised of all the families in the land', is Puritan humility and a paraphrase of the words of Old testament Gideon when he was called to be God's champion.

The Bunyans were a family of Norman-French origin (Buignon) who had owned land in north Bedfordshire as early as 1199. John's father, Thomas Bunyan, was a small landowner and blacksmith who reared his large family in a house well above the average size for Elstow.

John admits to an education, but makes disparaging remarks about it. The indications are, however, that his father paid for him to attend Bedford Grammar School. The fact that, following his military service (in Parliament's cause) at the garrison in Newport Pagnall, he returned to complete his apprenticeship as a brazier or blacksmith under his Anglican royalist father, lends credance to his story that he had wasted his substance with local hooligans. His education had prepared him for something better.

Bunyan's friendship with Matthias Cowley, who kept a stationer's or booksellers's shop in Newport Pagnall during his three years of soldiering, provided his opportunity to read the classics, including *Paradise Lost*. Nevertheless, the Authorised Version of the Bible, a love for which he acquired as the result of the sermons of Christopher Hall, vicar of Elstow, was the chief source of his continuing education. Bunyan's closely-argued exposition of Pauline theology to be found in *Pilgrim's Progress Part II* (1685), following Christiana's Calvary, would bear comparison with that of the great Independent theologian Dr. John Owen, Bunyan's friend and champion.

Legend has it that, during his 1660-1672 imprisonment, Bunyan had only the Bible and Fox's *Act and Monuments* for reading matter. However, in this period Bunyan published nine books, many of which strongly suggest a familiarity with the Elizabethan dramatists.

Bunyan's intense spiritual search began after his first marriage in 1648/9. Since he had yet to discover the letters of Paul, he set out to *achieve, deserve* salvation. As *Grace Abounding* portrays so graphically, at one moment he was on a high, proud of his new godliness, at another he was sucked under the Slough of Despond.

Having tried the road of legalism himself, Bunyan was well ready for Edward Fowler's legalistic attacks on his theology in the 1670s. Indeed Fowler was inserted into the second edition of *Pilgrim's Progress* (the first edition had been published in 1678) in the person of Mr. Worldly Wiseman. Modern commentators have interpreted Bunyan's strictures against this character, and that of his friend Mr. Legality (who lived on Mt. Sinai), as a Dickens-like attack on the legal profession. In fact it was his attack on 'the works of the law' as a means to salvation — he had tried that route himself — and a vivid illustration of justification by grace through faith in the Christ of Calvary.

Bunyan's encounter with Christ came through the ministry of John Gifford at St. Johns, Bedford in 1653. There is no record that Bunyan was baptized by immersion (parish records in Elstow indicate that his children were christened), and it is certain that Gifford's congregation was a Union church made up of both Baptists and Independents. Hence there is no ground whatever to assert, as so many have done, that Bunyan became a Baptist preacher. In his *Differences in Judgement about Water Baptism* (1673) he incurred the anger of prominent Baptists by arguing that adult baptism was a non-essential.

Through Gifford's ministry Bunyan experienced the new birth, a term which had first entered his vocabulary when he heard a group of women gossiping about their spiritual experience in Bedford marketplace. But Bunyan's new birth was not the end of troubles for him. As he became more and more captivated by the Gospel, he became more and more sensitive to his sins and failures. When he received the assurance of salvation it came like a bolt from the heavens; 'I saw . . . that it was not my good frame of heart that made my righteousness better, nor yet my bad frame that made my righteousness worse; for my righteousness was

Jesus Christ himself, the same yesterday, and today, and for ever.'

This realization liberated Bunyan from his obsession with his sins and prepared him to be the greatest popular preacher of his century. He was soon in great demand and, by the Restoration in 1660, had a standing that went beyond the boundaries of Bedfordshire. All told, he was to publish more than sixty works. His major works were *Grace Abounding* (1666), *Pilgrim's Progress Part 1* (1678), *The Life and Death of Mr. Badman.* (1680), *The Holy War* (1682), and *Pilgrim's Progress Part II* (1685). Apart from the occasional excursion into doctrinal debate the remainder of his works took the form of published sermons or amplified sermons. Some of these latter ran into between 75 and 100 pages. Among the best of these amplified sermons, all in a forceful, direct style, are *Come and Welcome to Jesus Christ* (1678), *The Barren Fig Tree* (1685), *The Jerusalem Sinner Saved* (1688), and *The Water of Life* (1688).

What established Bunyan's *national* reputation as a preacher and presented him with the opportunity to embark on his career as popular writer was his twelve-year imprisonment. In the years immediately prior to it his first wife had died leaving him four children, including blind Mary, who occupied a place especially close to his heart, his preaching and his regular work as a brazier placed a heavy strain upon him. The Bedford congregation advised him to remarry. He did. His second wife's name was Elizabeth. She was carrying their first child at the time of his arrest. The shock of the arrest caused her to miscarry.

We have no record as to how Bunyan viewed the Restoration of the Stuarts. Charles II's Declaration of Breda promised liberty to 'tender consciences'.

However, within three months of the king's landing at Dover, the Bedford meeting was turned out of St. Johns. In the years that followed they met in fields, woods, attics, and barns.

Bunyan's arrest came on 12 November 1660 while preaching at a house in Lower Samsell, midway between Bedford and Luton. The misnamed 'Clarendon Code' had not as yet been enacted; the Restoration Parliament did not meet until 8 May 1661. The laws under which Bunyan was arrested were 1 Elizabeth c. 2 and 35 Elizabeth c. 1. The first required all persons to resort to church every Sunday or face a fine. The second made frequenting conventicles punishable by imprisonment on the first offence, banishment on the second. This Elizabeth legislation had been aimed against Roman Catholics. In the years to come it would be used against Protestant Nonconformists. That the Bedfordshire magistracy was among the first to use it in this way, and that Bunyan was among the first to suffer, says something for Bunyan's reputation as well as for the zeal of the local magistracy in paying off old scores.

Bunyan's imprisonment was in the County Gaol on the corner of Silver Street and High Street, Bedford. Except for a brief break in 1666, Bunyan's imprisonment was continuous until Charles II's Declaration of Indulgence in 1672.

Elizabeth Bunyan made valiant efforts to free her husband, on one occasion travelling as fas as London. Gaolers varied in their severity. Local church books indicate that in the first year of his imprisonment Bunyan managed to secure an *exeat* for two or three hours on a Sunday (and that he used these opportunities to preach).

Periodically Bunyan was brought before the Quarter Sessions. The Chairman of the Sessions, Sir John Kelynge, found his way into *Pilgrim's Progress* as Lord Hategood of Vanity Fair. Others of his inflexible Tory judges found a dubious immortality as figures in Bunyan's other great allegory *The Holy War*, an account of the great controversy between good and evil that began in heaven, precipitated the fall of man, underlay all of human history, and led to the victory of righteousness at Calvary and a final intervention God's Son into cosmic history at the close of the age.

On Bunyan's release he secured a licence 'to teach as a Congregational Person' dated 9 May 1672. He was made pastor of the Bedford congregation. They acquired a building in which to meet. But Bunyan's preaching schedule took him to Hitchin, Luton, Cambridge, Reading, and London. Many new congregations of Nonconformists were established. In London Charles II, having heard that Dr. John Owen greatly admired Bunyan's preaching, asked the great scholar how he could sit and listen to an itinerant tinker. 'May it please Your Majesty,' replied Owen. 'I will gladly give up all all my learning for that tinker's power of preaching.'

In February 1675 Charles II revoked his Declaration of Indulgence. By 4 March a warrant was out for Bunyan's arrest. In 1660 he had done nothing to avoid arrest. This time he went underground. Constantly on the move and in hiding he continued to preach. Eventually he was taken up on a 'writ of *de excommunicato capiendo'*.

Again the old legal machinery was used against him, not the Uniformity, Five Mile or Conventicle Acts of the Restoration Parliament. Influential friends secured his release in June 1677. Part I of *Pilgrim's Progress* was now ready for the presses.

His last ten years of life were filled with preaching and writing. He took full advantage of the new freedom made possibly by James II's Declaration of Indulgence April 1687. However, when the Catholic king's electoral agents sought to elicit his support in the government's campaign to undermine the Church of England and pack a parliament, Bunyan refused to see them. In common with others he saw the Church of England as the great bastion of Protestantism.

Increasingly he preached in London, often in the halls of the great City Companies. 'When Mr. Bunyan preached in London,' reported Charles Doe, 'if there were but one day's notice given, there would be more people come together to hear him preach than the meeting-house could hold. I have been to hear him preach, by computation, about twelve hundred at a morning lecture by seven o'clock on a working day in the dark winter time.'

His death came in London on 31 August 1688 after a hard ride in the rain from Reading. On 3 September he was buried in Bunhill Fields.

In his time there was none to match him as a communicator of the Gospel by word of mouth or word of pen. His great appeal was to be accounted for by his common man's vocabulary (without the common man's grammar), his colourful imagination — and his intense desire to make the greatest of sinners (which he believed he himself had once been) understand that they could know salvation through the power of the Christian Gospel.

Samuel Taylor Coleridge spoke of 'the inimatable *Pilgrim's Progress,* that model of beautiful, pure, and harmonious English.' Part I went through eleven editions amounting to a hundred thousand copies in his lifetime, an enormous sale by seventeeth-century standards. Dr. Samuel Johnson left it on record that *The Pilgrim's Progress* was one of the few books that he could reread and reread. 'His *Pilgrim's Progress*', he said, 'has great merit, both for invention, imagination, and the conduct of the story; and it has the best evidence of its merit, the genral and continued approbation of mankind!' On the flyleaf of his copy of *The Pilgrim's Progress* Coleridge wrote, 'I know of no book, the Bible excepted as above all comparison, which I, according to my judgement and experience, could so safely recommend as teaching and enforcing the whole saving truth according to the mind that was in Christ Jesus, as *The Pilgrim's Progress.*'

Today we have no problems with Macaulay's assertion that John Bunyan was one of the two great creative minds in the second half of the seventeeth century. However, surely the really remarkable fact about Bunyan's work is that it continues to speak so clearly to the twentieth.

Selections from
Grace Abounding to the Chief of Sinners

(An account of Bunyan's spiritual odyssey, his converion, his call to a preaching ministry, and his imprisonment. Completed in 1666.)

For my descent, then, it was, as is well known by many, of a low and inconsiderable generation; my father's house being of that rank that is meanest and most despised of all the families in the land . . . .

Notwithstanding the meanness and inconsiderableness of my parents, it pleased God to put it into their hearts to put me to school, to learn both to read and write . . . .

Being filled with all unrighteousness . . . from a child, I had but few equals . . . both for cursing, swearing, lying, and blaspheming the holy name of God . . . In my childhood he did scare and afright me with fearful dreams, and did terrify me with dreadful visions; for often, after I had spent this and the other day in sin, I have in my bed been greatly afflicted, while asleep, with the apprehensions of devils and wicked spirits, who still, as I then thought, laboured to draw me away with them, of which I could never be rid. . . . These things, I say, when I was but a child, but nine or ten years old ... .

Awhile after, these terrible dreams did leave me . . .; wherefore, with more greediness, according to the strength of nature, I did still let loose the reins to my lusts, and delighted in all transgression against the law of God: so that, until I came to the state of marriage, I was the very ringleader of all the youth that kept me company, into all manner of vice and ungodliness . . . .

That God did not utterly leave me, but followed me still . . . . while I was a soldier, I, with others, were drawn out to go to such a place to besiege it; but when I was just ready to go, one of the company desired to go in my room; to which, when I had consented, he took my place; and coming to the siege, as he stood sentinel, he was shot into the head with a musket bullet, and died.

Here were judgements and mercy, but neither of them did awaken my soul to righteousness; wherefore I sinned still, and grew more and more rebellious against God, and careless of my own salvation . . . .

My mercy was to light upon a wife whose father was counted godly. This woman and I, though we came together as poor as poor might be, not having so much household stuff as a dish or spoon betwixt us both; yet this she had for her part, *The Plain Man's Pathway to Heaven,* and *The Practice of Piety,* which her father had left her when he died.

. . . I fell in very eagerly with the religion of the times, to wit, to go to church twice a day . . . I was not sensible of the danger and evil of sin . . . . (and) took much delight in all manner of vice . . . .

Though, as yet I was nothing but a poor painted hypocrite, yet I loved to be talked of as one that was truly godly. I was proud of my godliness, and, indeed, I did all I did, either to be seen of, or to be well spoken of, by man . . . . I was all this while ignorant of Jesus Christ, and going about to establish my own righteousness; and had perished therein had not God, in mercy, showed me more of my state of nature.

Upon a day, the good providence of god did cast me

to Bedford, to work on my calling; and in one of the streets of that town, I came where there were three or four poor women sitting at a door in the sun, and talking about the things of God; . . . their talk was about a new birth, the work of God in their hearts . . . They also . . . did sleight and abhor their own righteousness, as filthy and insufficient to do them any good. Methought they spake as if joy did make them speak; . . . They were to me, as if they had found a new world.

. . . I saw that in my thoughts about religion and salvation, the new birth did never enter into my mind, neither knew I the comfort of the Word and promise, nor the deceitfulness and treachery of my own wicked heart. . . . I was greatly affected with their words.

. . . And now, methought, I began to look into the Bible with new eyes, and read as I never did before; and especially the epistles of the apostle Paul . . . .

I should pray wherever I was, whether at home or abroad, in house or field; . . . but instead of having satisfaction, here I began to find my soul to be assaulted with fresh doubts about my future happiness; especially with such as these, Whether I was elected? . . . For, thought I, if I be not called, what then can do me good? None but those who are effectually called, inherit the kingdom of heaven. But oh! how I now loved those words that spake of a Christian's calling! as when the Lord said to one, 'Follow me' and to another, 'Come after me,' and oh! thought I that he would say so to me too, how gladly would I run after him! I cannot now express with what longings and breakings in my soul I cried to Christ to call me . . . .

About this time I began to break my mind to those poor people in Bedford, and to tell them my condition, which, when they had heard, they told Mr. Gifford of me, who himself also took occasion to talk with me, and was willing to be well persuaded of me, though I think but from little grounds ...

Now I evidently found that lusts and corruptions would strongly put forth themselves within me, in wicked thoughts and desires .... Now I grow worse and worse; now am I further from conversion than ever I was before ....

But all this while as to the act of sinning, I never was more tender than now. ... But, I observed, though I was such a great sinner before conversion, yet God never much charged the guilt of the sins of my ignorance upon me; only he showed me I was lost if I had not Christ, because I had been a sinner; I saw that I wanted a perfect righteousness to present me without fault before God, and this righteouness was nowhere to be found, but in the person of Jesus Christ.

... If my guilt lay hard upon me, then I should cry that the blood of Christ might take it off; ... 'Without shedding of blood is no remission.' Hebrews 9:22 .... Then I began to give place to the word, ... Nothing shall separate thee from my love. ... Now was my heart filled full with comfort and hope, and now I could believe that my sins should be forgiven me. ...

For about the space of a month after, a very great storm came down upon me, which handled me twenty times worse than all I had met with before; it came stealing upon me, now by one piece, then by another; first, all my comfort was taken from me, then darkness seized upon me, after which, whole floods of blasphemies, both against God, Christ, and the scriptures, were poured upon my spirit, to my great confusion and astonishment .... While this temptation lasted, which was about a year, I could attend upon none of the ordinances of God but with sore and great affliction. . . . In prayer, also, I had been greatly troubled at this time; sometime I have thought I should see the devil, nay, thought I have felt him, behind me . . . . Yet, at times I should have some strong and heart-affecting apprehensions of God, and the reality of the truth of his gospel . . . .

I had, also, one sweet glance from second Corinthians 5:21: 'For he that made him to be sin for us, who knew no sin; that we might be made the righteousness of God in him.' I remember, also, that one day as I was sitting in my neighbour's house, and there very sad at the consideration of my many blasphemies, and as I was saying in my mind, What ground have I to think that I, who have been so vile and abomonable, should ever inherit eternal life? that Word came suddenly upon me, 'what shall we say to these things? if God before us, who can be against us?' Romans 8:31 . . . .

At this time, also, I sat under the ministry of holy Mr. Gifford, whose doctrine, by God's grace, was much for my stablility . . . . Then began I with sad careful heart, to consider of the nature and largeness of my sin, and to search in the word of God, if I could in any place espy a word of promise, or any encouraging sentence by which I might take relief. Wherefore I began to consider that third of Mark, All manner of sins and blasphemies shall be forgiven unto the sons of men . . . .

But my temptations, at all times, came hard upon me. Here I should consider the sin of David, of Solomon, of Manasseh, of Peter, and of the rest of the great offenders; and should also labour, what might with fairness, to aggravate and heighten their sins by several circumstances: but alas! it was all in vain.

I should think with myself that David shed blood to cover his adultery, and that by the sword of the children of Ammon; a work that could not be done but by continuance and deliberate contrivance, which was a great aggravation to his sin. But then this would turn upon me: Ah! but these were but sins against the law, from which there was a Jesus sent to save them; but yours is a sin against the Saviour, and who shall save you from that!

... Now I should find my mind to flee from God, as from the face of the dreadful judge; yet this was my torment, I could not escape his hand: 'It is a fearful thing to fall into the hands of the living God.' Hebrews 10:31 ... But it would come into my mind, when I was fleeing from the face of God ... 'Return unto me; for I have redeemed thee.' I could discern that the God of grace did follow me a pardon in his hand ....

Once as I was walking to and fro in a good man's shop ... lamenting this hard hap of mine, for that I should commit so great a sin, greatly fearing I should not be pardoned; praying, also, in my heart, this sin of mine did differ from that against the Holy Ghost, the Lord would show me. And being now ready to sink with fear, suddenly, there was, as if there had rushed in at the window, the noise of wind upon me, but very pleasant, and as if I heard a voice speaking, Didst ever refuse to be justified by the blood of Christ? ... It showed me that Jesus Christ had yet a word of grace and mercy for me, that he had not, as I had feared, quite forsaken and cast off my soul ..... Only this I say, it commanded a great calm in my soul, it persuaded me there might be hope; it showed me, as I thought, that the sin unpardonable was, and that my soul had yet the blessed privilege to flee to Jesus Christ for mercy ....

But, oh! it was hard for me to bear the face to pray to this Christ for mercy, against whom I had thus most vilely sinned; . . . But I saw there was but one way with me, I must go to him and humble myself unto him and beg that he, of his wonderful mercy, would show pity to me, and have mercy upon my wretched sinful soul.

Which, then the tempter perceived, he strongly suggested to me, That I ought not to pray to God; for prayer was not for any in my case, neither could it do me good. . . . Thus, by the strange and unusual assaults of the tempter, was my soul, like a broken vessel, driven as with the winds, and tossed sometimes headlong into despair, sometimes upon the covenant of works . . . .

So one day I walked to a neighbouring town, and sat down upon a settle in the street . . .. Breaking out in the bitterness of my soul, I said to myself, with a grievous sigh, How can God comfort such a wretch as I? I had no sooner said it but this returned upon me, as an echo doth answer a voice, This sin is not unto death . . . Now, thought I, if this sin is not unto death, then it is pardonable; therefore, from this I have encouragement to come to God by Christ, for mercy. . . . None but those that know what my trouble, by their own experience, was, can tell what relief came to my soul by this consideration; it was a release to me from my former bonds, and a shelter from my former storm . . .

The tempter again laid at me very sore, suggesting, That neither the mercy of God, nor yet the blood of Christ, did at all concern me, nor could they help me for my sin. . . . But one morning, when I was again at prayer, a piece of a sentence darted in upon me, 'My grace is sufficient'. . . . Therefore I prayed to God that he would come in with this scripture more fully on my heart; to wit, that he would help me to apply the whole sentence for as yet I could not . . . .

One day I was in a meeting of God's people, full of sadness and terror, my fears again were strong upon me; and I was now thinking my soul was never the better, but my case most sad and fearful, these words did, with great power, suddenly break in upon me, 'My grace is sufficient for thee, my grace is sufficient for thee, my grace is sufficient for thee,' three times together; and, oh! methought that every word was a mighty word unto me; as *my*, and *grace*, and *sufficient*, and *for thee* . . . .. It broke my heart, and filled me full of joy . . . .

This scripture did also most sweetly visit my soul, 'And him that cometh to me I will in no wise cast out.' John 6:37. Oh, the comfort that I have had from this word, 'in no wise,' as who should say, by no means, for no thing, whatever he hath done . . . .

But the temptations continued as before . . . .

One day, as I was passing in the field, fearing lest yet all was not right, suddenly this sentence fell upon my soul, Thy righteousness is in heaven; and methought withall, I saw, with the eyes of my soul, Jesus Christ at God's right hand; there, I say, as my righteousness; so that wherever I was, or whatever I was adoing, God could not say of me, He wants my righteousness, for that was just before him. I also saw moreover, that it was not my good frame of heart that made my righteousness better, nor yet my bad frame that made my righteousness worse; for my righteousness was Jesus Christ himself, the same yesterday, and today, and forever.

Now did my chains fall off my legs indeed; I was loosed from my afflication and irons, my temptation fled away . . . . Now Christ was all; all my wisdom, all my righteousness, all my sanctification, and all my redemption.

Further, the Lord did also lead me into the mystery of union with Son of God, that I was joined to him, that I was flesh of his flesh . . . . By this also was my faith in him, as my righteousness, the more confirmed to me; for if he and I were one, then his righteousness was mine, his merits mine, his victory mine.

Selections from
The Holy War

The Fall Of Mansoul

In my travels . . . it was my chance to happen into the famous continent of Universe . . . It lieth between the two poles, and just amidst the four points of the heavens . . .

There is in this gallant country of Universe, a fair and delicate town, a corporation called Mansoul . . . . The first founder and builder of it . . . was one Shaddai (Genesis 1:26) . . . .

There was reared up in the midst of this town a most famous and stately palace . . . . This place the King Shaddai intended but for himself . . . .

Mansoul had five gates in it . . . . The names of the gates were these: Ear-gate, Eye-gate, Mouth-gate, Nose-gate, and Feel-gate . . . . There was not a rascal, rogue, or traitorous person then within its walls; they were all true men, and fast joined together . . .

Well, upon a time, there was one Diabolus, a mighty giant, made an assault upon his famous town of Mansoul, to take it, and make it his own habitation. As to his origin, Diabolus was at first one of the servants of King Shaddai, made, and taken and put by him into most high and mighty place; . . . It brought him much glory, and gave him much brightness, as income that might have contented his Luciferian heart, had it not been insatiable, and enlarged as hell itself.

Well, he seeing himself thus exalted to greatness and honour, and raging in his mind for higher state and degree, what doth he but begin to think with himself that how he might be set up as lord over all, and have the sole power under Shaddai. (Now that did the King reserve for his Son, yea, and had already bestowed it upon him.) Wherefore he first consults with himself what had best to be done; and then breaks his mind to some other of his companions, to the which they also agreed. So, in fine, they came to this issue, that they should make an attempt upon the king's son to destroy him, that the inheritance might be theirs . . . .

Now the King and his Son, being all and always, eye, could not but discern all passages in his dominions; and he, having always love for his Son as for himself, could not at what he saw but be greatly provoked and offended; wherefore . . . he cast them altogether out of all place of trust, benefit, honour, and preferment. This done, he banished them the court . . . .

Now they being thus cast out . . . , you may be sure they would now add to their former pride what malice and rage against Shaddai and against his Son, they could. Wherefore, roving and ranging in much fury from place to place . . . they happened into this spacious country of Universe, and steer their course towards the town of Mansoul; and considering that that town was one of the chief works and delights of King Shaddai, what do they but, after counsel taken, make as assault upon that. 'Now we have found the prize, and how to be revenged on King Shaddai for what he hath done to us.'

. . . .'It is impossible,' said Diabolus, 'that we should take the town: for that none can enter into it without its own consent. Let, therefore, but few, all but one, assault Mansoul; and in mine opinion, let me be he.' Wherefore, to this they all agreed . . . .

Then considered they whether they had not best to give out orders to some of their company to shoot someone or more of the principal of the townsmen . . . . This was carried in the affirmative, and the man that was designed by this strategem to be destroyed was one Mr. Resistance, otherwise called Captain Resistance. And a great man in Mansoul this Captain Resistance was, and a man that the giant Diabolus and his band more feared than they feared the whole town of Mansoul beside . . . .

They marched towards Mansoul . . . . They drew up, and sat down before the Ear-gate. The giant ascended up close to the gate, and called the town of Mansoul for audience . . .; at which the chief of the town of Mansoul, such as my Lord Innocent, my Lord Will-be-will, my Lord Mayor, Mr. Recorder and Captain Resistance, came down to the wall to see who was there . . .

Diabolus, then, as if he had been a lamb, began his oration and said, 'Gentlemen of the famous town of Mansoul, I am, as you may perceive, no far dweller from you, but near, and one that is bound by the King to do you my homage and what service I can; wherefore, that I may be faithful to myself, and to you, I have somewhat of concern to impart unto you. Wherefore, grant me your audience, and hear me patiently. And first, I will assure you, it is not myself, but you — not mine, but your advantage I seek by what I now do, as will full well be made manifest, by that I have opened my mind unto you. For, gentlemen, I am (to tell you the truth) come to show you how you may obtain great and ample deliverance from a bondage that, unwares to yourselves, you are

25

captivated and enslaved under.' At this the town of Mansoul began to prick up its ears. And 'What is it? Pray what is it?' thought they. And he said, 'I have somewhat to say to you concerning your King, concerning his law, and also touching yourselves. Touching your King, I know he is great and potent; but yet all that he hath said to you is neither true nor yet to your advantage. It is not true, for that wherewith he hath hitherto awed you shall not come to pass, nor be fulfilled. . . . Touching his laws, this I say further, they are both unreasonable, intricate, and intolerable . . . Why should you be holden in ignorance and blindness? Why should you not be enlarged in knowledge and understanding? And now, oh ye inhabitants of the famous town of Mansoul, to speak more particulary to yourselves, you are not a free people! . . . . That very thing which you are forbidden to do, might you do it, would yield you both wisdom and honour — for then your eyes will be opened, and you shall be as gods . . . .

Just now, while Diabolus was speaking these words to Mansoul, Tisiphone shot at Captain Resistance, where he stood on the gate, and mortally wounded him on the head; so that he, to the amazement of the townsmen, and the encouragement of Diabolus, fell down dead . . . . The matter turned upon a tree . . . . When the townsfolk saw that the tree was good for food, and that it was pleasant to the eye, and a tree to be desired to make one wise . . . they took and did eat thereof . . . . My Lord Innocency . . . sunk down in the place where he stood, nor could he be brought to life again. Thus these two brave men died . . . .

When the men of Mansoul were taken with the forbidden fruit and did eat . . . they became immediately drunken therewith. So they opened the gate, both

Ear-gate and Eye-gate, and let in Diabolus with all his bands, quite forgetting their good Shaddai, his law . . . .

Diabolus, having now obtained entrance in at the gates of the town, marches up to the middle thereof, to make his conquest as sure as he could . . . . Then they all with one consent said, 'Do thou reign over us.' So he accepted the motion, and became the king of the town of Mansoul. This being done, the next thing was, to give him possession of the castle, and so of the whole strength of the town . . . .

Not thinking himself yet secure enough, in the next place he bethinks himself of new modelling the town; and so does, setting up one, and putting down another at pleasure. Wherefore, my Lord Mayor, whose name was My Lord Understanding, and Mr. Recorder, whose name was Mr. Conscience, these he put out of place and power.

As for my Lord Mayor, though he was an under-standing man, and one too that had complied with the rest of the town of Mansoul in admitting the giant into the town; yet Diabolus though not fit to let him abide in his former lustre and glory, because he was a seeing man. Wherefore he darkened him, not only by taking from his office and power, but by building an high and strong tower, just between the sun's reflections and the windows of my Lord's palace; by which means his house and all, and the whole of his habitation, were made as dark as darkness itself. And thus, being alienated from the light, he became as one that was born blind. To this his house, my Lord was confined as to a prison; nor might he, upon his parole, go farther than within his own bounds . . .

As for Mr. Recorder, before the town was taken, he was a man well read in the laws of his King, and also a man of courage and faithfulness to speak truth at every occasion; and he had a tongue as bravely hung, as he had a head filled with judgement. Now, this man Diabolus could by no means abide, because, though he gave his consent to his coming into the town, yet he could not, by all the whiles, trials, strategems, and devices that he could use, make him wholly his own. True, he was degenerated from his former King, . . . but he would now and then think upon Shaddai . . .; and therefore the now king of Mansoul could not abide him.

Diabolus therefore feared the recorder more than any that was left alive in the town of Mansoul, because . . . his words did shake the whole town . . . . Since, therefore, the giant could not make him wholly his own, what doth he do but studies all that he could to debauch the old gentleman, and by debauchery to stupify his mind, and more harden his heart in the ways of vanity. And as he attempted, so he accomplished his design: he debauched the man, and, by little, and little so drew him into sin and wickedness, that at last he was not only debauched, as at first, and so by consequence defiled, but was almost past all conscience of sin. And this was the farthest Diabolus could go . . . .

By one means or another, he quickly got Mansoul to sleight, neglect, and despise whatever Mr. Recorder could say . . . . And when Mansoul *did* used to be frighted with the thundering voice of the Recorder, and when they did tell Diabolus of it, he would answer that what the old gentleman said was neither of love to him nor pity to them, but of a foolish fondness that he had to be prating; and so would hush, still, and put all to quiet again. And that he might leave no argument unurged that might tend to make them secure, he said, and said it often, 'Oh Mansoul! consider that, notwith-standing the old gentleman's rage, and the rattle of his high and thundering words, you hear nothing of Shaddai himself.... You see that he values not the loss nor rebellion of the town of Mansoul, nor will he trouble himself with calling his town to a reckoning for they giving themselves to me. He knows that though you were his, now you are lawfully mine; so, leave us one to another, he now hath shaken his hands of us.'

Shaddai's Plan To Recapture Mansoul

And now Diabolus thought himself safe. He had taken Mansoul, he had engarrisoned himself therein; he had put down the old officers, and had set up new ones; he had defaced the image of Shaddai, and set up his own; he had spoiled the old law books, and had promoted his own vain lies; he had made his own new magistrates, and set up new aldermen; he had builded him new holds, and had manned them for himself; and all this he did to make himself secure, in case the good Shaddai, or his Son, should come to make an incursion upon him ....

The King and his son foresaw all this long before, yea, and sufficiently provided for the relief of Mansoul .... Thus gave they conviction to all about them that they had love and compassion for the famous town of Mansoul. Well, when the King and his Son were retired into the privy chamber, there they again consulted about what they had designed before, to wit, that as Mansoul should in time be suffered to be lost, so as certainly it should be recovered again .... Wherefore, after this consult, the Son of Shaddai (a sweet and comely Person, and one that had always great affection for those that were in affliction ...) — this Son of Shaddai, I say, having stricken hands with his father, and promised that he would be his servant to recover his Mansoul again, stood by his resolution, nor would he repent of the same.

The purport of this agreement was this: to wit, that at a certain time, prefixed by both, the King's Son should take a journey into the country of Universe, and there, in a way of justice and equity, by making amends for the follies of Mansoul, he should lay a foundation of a perfect deliverance from Diabolus and from his tyranny ....

Selections from
Pilgrim's Progress

The City Of Destruction, Mount Sinai And The Cross

As I walked through the wilderness of this world I lighted on a certain place where there was a den, and laid me down in that place to sleep; and, as I slept, I dreamed a dream. I dreamed, and behold, I saw a man clothed with rages standing in a certain place, with his face from his own house, a book in his hand and a great burden upon his back. I looked, and saw him open the book, and read therein; and, as he read, he wept and trembled; and, not being able longer to contain, he broke out with a lamentable cry, saying, 'What shall I do?'. . .

Now I saw, upon a time, when he was walking in the fields, that he was (as he was wont) reading in his book, and greatly distressed in his mind; and, as he read, he burst out, as he had done before, crying, 'What shall I do to be saved?'

I saw, also, that he looked this way and that way, as if would run; yet he stood still, because (as I perceived) he could not tell which way to go. I looked then, and saw a man named Evangelist coming to him, and asked, Wherefore dost thou cry?

He answered, Sir, I perceive, by the book in my hand, that I am condemned to die, and after that to come to judgement; and I find that I am not willing to do the first, nor able to do the second.

Then said Eveangelist, Why not willing to die, since this life is attended with so many evils? The man answered, Because I fear that this burden that is upon my back will sink me lower than the grave . . . .

Evangelist pointing with his finger over a very wide field, Do you see yonder Wicket-gate? The man said, No. Then said the other, Do you see yonder shining light? He said, I think I do. Then said Evangelist, Keep that light in your eye, and go up directly thereto, so shalt thou see the gate; at which, when thou knockest, it shall be told thee what thou shalt do. So I saw in my dream that the man began to run. . . .

Now . . . he espied one afar off, come crossing over the field to meet him; and their hap was to meet just as they were crossing the way of each other. The gentleman's name that met him was Mr. Worldly Wiseman: he dwelt in the town of Carnal Policy; A very great town, and also hard by from whence Christian eame. This man, then, meeting with Christian, and having some inkling of him — for Christian setting forth from the City of Destruction was much noised abroad, not only in the town where he dwelt, but also it began to be the town-talk in some other places — Mr. Worldly Wiseman, therefore, having some guess of him, by beholding his laborious going, by observing his sighs and groans, and the like, began thus to enter into some talk with Christian.

Worldly Wiseman: How now, good fellow; whither away after this burdened manner;

Christian: A burdened manner indeed, as ever, I think, poor creature had! . . . I tell you, sir, I am going to yonder Wicket-gate before me; for there, as I am

32

informed, I shall be put into a way to be rid of my heavy burden. . . .

    Worldy Wiseman: Wilt thou hearken to me if I give thee counsel?

    Christian: If it be good, I will; for I stand in need of good counsel . . .

Worldly Wiseman: Hear me; I am older than thou: thou art like to meet with, in the way which thou goest, wearisomeness, painfulness, hunger, perils, nakedness, sword, lions, dragons, darkness, and, in a word, death and whatnot. . . . In yonder village (the village is named Morality) there dwells a gentleman whose name is Legality, a very judicious man, and a man of a very good name, that has skill to help men off with such burdens as thine is from their shoulders . . . .

Now was Christian somewhat at a stand; but presently he concluded, If this be true which this gentleman hath said, my wisest course is to take his advice . . . .

    Christian: Sir, which is my way to this honest man's house?

    Worldly Wiseman: Did you see yonder high hill?

    Christian: Yes, very well.

    Worldly Wiseman: By that hill you must go . . . .

So Christian turned out of his way to go to Mr. Legality's house for help. But, behold, when he was got now hard by the hill, it seemed so high, and also that side of it that was next the wayside did hang so much over, that Christian was afraid to venture farther, lest the hill should fall on his head; wherefore, there he stood still, and wotted not what to do. Also his burden now seemed heavier to him than while he was in his way. There came also flashes of fire out of the hill, that made Christian afraid that he should be burned; here, therefore, he did sweat and quake for fear. . . . He saw Evangelist coming to meet him, at the sight also of whom he began to blush for shame . . . .

Evangelist: What dost thou here, Christian? said he . . . . Did not I direct thee the way to the little Wicket-gate? . . . How is it, then, that thou art so quickly turned aside? For thou art now out of the way.

Then said Evangelist, Stand still a little, that I may show thee the words of God. So he stood trembling. Then said Evangelist, . . . 'Now the just shall live by faith' . . ., 'All manner of sin and blasphemies shall be forgiven unto men', 'Be not faithless, but believing'.

The man that met thee is one Worldy Wiseman, and rightly is he so called; partly because he savoureth only of the doctrine of this world — therefore he always goes to the town of Morality to church; and partly because he loveth that doctrine best, for it savest him best from the cross . . . .

He to whom thou wast sent for ease, by name Legality . . . (lives on) Mount Sinai, which thou hast feared will fall on thy head . . . . This Legality, therefore, is not able to set thee free from thy burden. No man was yet ever rid of his burden by him, no, nor ever is like to be. Ye cannot be justified by the works of the law; for by the deeds of the law no man living can be rid of his burden; therefore, Mr. Worldly Wiseman is an alien, and Mr. Legality is a cheat . . . .

Then did Christian address himself to go back; Evangelist, after he had kissed him, gave him one smile, and bid him God-speed . . . .

Now I saw in my dream that the highway up which Christian was to go, was fenced on either side with a wall, and that wall was Salvation. Up this way, therefore, did burdened Christian run, but not without great difficulty, because of the load on his back.

He ran thus till he came to a place somewhat ascending; and upon that place stood a Cross, and a little below, in the bottom, a Sepulchre. So I saw in my dream, that just as Christian came up with the Cross, his burden loosed from off his shoulders, and fell from off his back, and began to tumble, and so continued to do, till it came to the mouth of the Sepulchre, where it fell in, and I saw it no more.

Then was Christian glad and lightsome, and said, with a merry heart, He hath given me rest by His sorrow, and life by His death. . . . Then Christian gave three leaps for joy, and went on singing —

> Thus far did I come ladened with my sin,
> Nor could aught ease the grief that I was in,
> Till I came hither, What a place is this!
> Must here be the beginning of my bliss?
> Must here the burden fall off from my back?
> Must here the strings that bound it to me crack?
> Blest Cross! Blest Sepulchre! Blest, rather be,
> The Man that there was put to shame for me!

Giant Despair And Doubting Castle

Now I saw in my dream that Christian went not forth alone; for there was one whose name was Hopeful . . . who joined himself unto him, and, entering into a brotherly covenant, told him that he would be his companion . . . .

I saw then that they went on their way to a pleasant river, which David the king called 'the river of God', but John, 'the river of the water of life'. Now their way lay just upon the bank of this river: here, therefore, Christian and his companion walked with great delight; they drank also of the water of the river, which was pleasant and enlivening to their weary spirit . . . .

Now, I beheld in my dream, that they had not journeyed far, but the river and the way for a time parted, at which they were not a little sorry; yet they durst not go out of the way. Now the way from the river was rough, and their feet tender by reason of their travel; so the souls of the pilgrims were much discouraged because of the way. Wherefore, still as they went on they wished for a better way. Now, a little before them, there was on the left hand of the road a meadow, and a stile to go over into it; and that meadow is called By-path Meadow. Thus said Christian to his fellow, If this meadow lieth along by our wayside, let us go over into it. Then he went to the stile to see, and behold, a path lay along by the way on the other side of the fence. 'Tis according to my wish, said Christian; here is the easiest going; come, good Hopeful, and let us go over.

Hopeful: But how if this path should lead us out of the way?

Christian: That is not likely . . . . Look, doth it not go along by the wayside?

So Hopeful, being persuaded by his fellow, went after him over the stile. When they were gone over, and were got into the path, they found it very easy for their feet; and withall, they, looking before them, espied a man walking as they did, and his name was Vain-confidence: so they called after him, and asked him whither that way led. He said, To the Celestial Gate. Look, said Christian, did not I tell you so? By this you may see we are right. So they followed, and they went before them. But, behold, the night came on, and it grew very dark; so that they were behind lost sight of him that went before.

He therefore that went before (Vain-confidence by name), not seeing the way before him, fell into a deep pit, which was on purpose there ... to catch vain-glorious fools withal, and was dashed in pieces with his fall.

Now Christian and his fellow heard him fall; so they called to know the matter; but there was none to answer, only they heard a groaning. Then said Hopeful, Where are we now? Then was his fellow silent, as mistrusting that he had led him out of the way; and now it began to rain, and thunder, and lighten, in a most dreadful manner, and the water rose amain.

Then Hopeful groaned within himself, saying, Oh that I had kept on my way!

Christian: Who could have thought that this path should have led us out of the way?

Hopeful: I was afraid on it at the very first, and therefore gave you that gentle caution. I would have spoken plainer, but that you are older than I.

Christian: Good brother, be not offended; I am sorry I have brought thee out of the way, and that I have put thee into such imminent danger; pray, my brother, forgive me; I did not do it of an evil intent.

Hopeful: Be comforted, my brother, for I forgive thee; and I believe, too, that this shall be for our good.

Christian: I am glad I have with thee a merciful brother: but we must not stand here; let us try to go back again.

Hopeful But, good brother, let me go before.

Christian: No, if you please, let me go first, that if there be any danger, I may be first therein; because by my means we are both gone out of the way . . . .

They adventured to go back; but it was so dark, and the flood so high, that in their going back they had like to have been drowned nine or ten times.

Neither could they, with all the skill they had, get again to the stile that night. Wherefore, at last, lighting under a little shelter, they sat down there until daybreak; but, being weary, they fell asleep. Now there was, not far from the place where they lay, a castle, called Doubting Castle, and the owner thereof was Giant Despair; and it was in his grounds they now were sleeping. Wherefore he, caught Christian and Hopeful asleep in his grounds. Then, with a grim and surly voice, he bid them awake and asked them whence they were, and what they did in his grounds. They told him they were pilgrims, and that they had lost their way. Then said the giant, You have this night trespassed on me, by trampling in and lying on my grounds, and therefore you must go along with me. So they were forced to go, because he was stronger than they. They also had but little to say, for they knew themselves in a fault. The giant, therefore, drove them before him, and put them into his castle, in a very dark dungeon, nasty and stinking to the spirits of these two men. Here, then, they lay from Wednesday morning till Saturday night, without one bit of bread, or drop of drink, or light, or any to ask how they did; they were, therefore, here in evil case, and were far from friends and acquaintance. Now in this place Christian had double sorrow, because it was through his unadvised counsel that they were brought into this distress.

Now Giant Despair had a wife, and her name was Diffidence: so, when he was gone to bed, he told his wife what he had done; to wit, that he had taken a couple of prisoners, and cast them into his dungeon for trespassing on his ground. Then he asked her also what he had best do further to them. So she asked him what they were, whence they came, and whither they were bound; and he told her. Then she counselled him, that when he arose in the morning he should beat them without mercy. So when he arose, he getteth him a grievous crab-tree cudgel, and goes down into the dungeon to them, and there first falls to rating on them, as if they were dogs, although they never gave him a word of distaste: then he fell upon them, and beat them fearfully, in such sort that they were not able to help themselves, or to turn them upon the floor. This done he withdraws, and leaves them there to console their misery, and to mourn under their distress: so all that day they spent their time in nothing but sighs and bitter lamentations. The next night she, talking with her husband further about them, and understanding that they were yet alive, did advise him to counsel them to make away with themselves. So, when morning was come, he goes to them in a surly manner as before, and perceiving them to be very sore with the stripes that he had given them the day before, he told them, that since they were never like to come out of that place, their way only would be forthwith to make an end of themselves, either with knife, halter, or poison: For why, said he, should you chose to live, seeing it is attended with so much bitterness? But they desired him to let them go. With that he looked ugly upon them, and rushing to them, had doubtless made an end of them himself, but that he fell into one of his fits (for he sometimes, in sunshiny weather, fell into fits), and lost for a time the use of his hands; therefore he withdrew, and left them, as before, to consider what

to do. Then did the prisoners consult between themselves, whether it was best to take his counsel or no
. . . .

Christian: Brother . . . what shall we do? . . . . The grave is more easy for me than this dungeon! Shall we be ruled by the giant?

Hopeful: Indeed, our present condition is dreadful, and death would be far more welcome to me than thus forever to abide . . . . (But) others, so far as I can understand, have been taken by him as well as we, and yet have escaped out of his hand. Who knows but that God, who made the world, may cause that Giant Despair may die, or that, at some time or other, he may forget to lock us in; or that he may in a short time have another of his fits before us, and may lose the use of his limbs? . . . . Let us be patient, and endure a while: the time may come that may give us a happy release . . . .

Well, towards evening the giant goes down into the dungeon again, to see if his prisoners had taken his counsel; but when he came there, he found them alive; and, truly, alive was all, for now, what for want of bread and water, and by reason of the wounds they received when he beat them, they could do little but breathe. But, I say, he found them alive; at which he fell into a grievous rage, and told them that seeing they had disobeyed his counsel, it should be worse with them than if they had never been born.

At this they trembled greatly, and I think that Christian fell into a swoon; but, coming a little to himself again, they renewed their discourse about the giant's counsel, and whether yet they had best take it or no. Now Christian again seemed for doing it, but Hopeful made this second reply:-

Hopeful: My brother . . . rememberest thou not how

valiant thou hast best been heretofore? Apollyon could not crush thee, nor could all that thou didst hear, or see, or feel, in the Valley of the Shadow of Death. What hardship terror, and amazement hast thou already gone through, and art thou nothing but fears? .... Remember how thou playedst the man at Vanity Fair, and was neither afraid of the chain nor cage, nor yet of bloody death: wherefore, let us bear up with patience as well as we can.

Now, night being come again, and the giant and his wife being in bed, she asked him concerning the prisoners, and if they had taken his counsel: to which he replied, They are sturdy rogues, they choose rather to bear all hardship than to make away with themselves. Then said she, Take them into the castle-yard tomorrow, and show them the bones and skulls that thou hast already despatched, and make them believe, ere the week comes to an end, thou wilt tear them in pieces, as thou hast done their fellows before them.

So when the morning was come, the giant goes to them again, and takes them into the castle-yard, and shows them as his wife had bidden him. These, said he, were pilgrims, as you are, once, and they trespassed on my grounds, as you have done; and when I thought fit, I tore them in pieces; and so within ten days I will do you. Get you down to your den again: and with that he beat them all the way thither. They lay, therefore, all day on Saturday in a lamentable case, as before. Now when night was come, and when Mrs. Diffidence and her husband the giant were got to bed, they began to renew their discourse of the prisoners; and, withal, the old giant wondered that he could neither by this blows nor counsel bring them to an end. And with that his wife replied: I fear ... that they live in hopes that some will come to relieve them, or that they have picklocks about them, by the means of which they hope to escape. And sayest thou so, my dear? said the giant; I will therefore search them in the morning.

Well, on Saturday, about midnight, they began to pray, and continued in prayer till almost break of day.

Now a little before it was day, good Christian, as one half amazed, break out into this passionate speech: What a fool am I, thus to lie in a stinking dungeon, when I may as well walk at liberty! I have a key in my bosom called Promise, that will, I am persuaded, open any lock in Doubting Castle. Then said Hopeful, That's good news, good brother, pluck it out of thy bosom, and try.

Then Christian pulled it out of his bosom, and began to try at the dungeon door, whose bolt, as he turned the key, gave back, and the door flew open with ease, and Christian and Hopeful both came out. Then he went to the outward door that leads into the castle yard, and with his key opened that door also. After that, he went to the iron gate, for that must be opened too, but that lock went desperately hard; yet the key did open it. Then they thrust open the gate to make their escape with speed; but that gate, as it opened, made such a creaking, that it waked Giant Despair who, hastily rising to pursue his prisoners, felt his limbs to fail, for his fits took him again so that he could by no means go after them. Then they went on, and came to the King's highway again, and so were safe, because they were out of his jurisdiction. . . .

The Last Enemy

Now I saw in my dream, that by this time the pilgrims were . . . entering into the country of Beulah, whose air was very sweet and pleasant; the way was lying directly through it, they solaced themselves there for a season. Yea, here they heard continually the singing of birds, and saw every day the flowers appear in the earth, and heard the voice of the turtle in the land. In this country the sun shineth night and day: wherefore this was beyond the Valley of the Shadow of Death, and also out of the reach of Giant Despair; neither could they from this place so much as see Doubting Castle. Here they were within sight of the City they were going to: also here met them some of the inhabitants thereof; for in this land the Shining Ones commonly walked, because it was upon the borders of heaven . . . .

Now, as they walked in this land, they had more rejoicing than in parts more remote from the kingdom to which they were bound; and drawing near to the City, they had yet a more perfect view thereof. It was builded of pearls and precious stones, also the streets thereof were paved with gold . . . .

They walked on their way, and came yet nearer and nearer, where were orchards, vineyards, and gardens, and their gates opened into the highway. . . . So I saw that, as they went on, there met them two men in raiment that shone like gold, also their faces shone as the light.

These men asked the pilgrims whence they came; and they told them. They also asked them where they had lodged, what difficulties and dangers, what comforts and pleasures, they had met in the way; and they told them. Then said the men that met them, You have but two difficulties more to meet with, and then you are in the City.

Christian, then, and his companion asked the men to go along with them: so they told them that they would. But, said they, you must obtain it by your own faith. So I saw in my dream that they went on together till they came in sight of the gate.

Now I further saw, that between them and the gate was a river; but there was no bridge to go over; and the river was very deep. At the sight, therefore, of this river, the pilgrims were much stunned; but the men that went with them said, You must go through, or you cannot come at the gate.

The pilgrims then began to inquire if there was no other way to the gate? To which they answered, Yes; but there hath not any, save two, to wit, Enoch and Elijah ... being permitted to tread that path since the foundation of the world, nor shall until the last trumpet shall sound. The pilgrims then, especially Christian, began to despond, and looked this way and that; but could find no way by which they might escape the river. Then they asked the men if the waters were all the same depth? They said, No; yet they could not help them in that case; for, said they, you shall find it deeper or shallower, as you believe in the King of the place.

Then they addressed themselves to the water, and entering, Christian began to sink; and, crying out to his good friend Hopeful, he said, 'I sink in deep waters; the billows go over my head ...'.

Then said the other, Be of good cheer, my brother; I feel the bottom, and it is good. Then said Christian, Ah! my friend, 'the sorrows of death hath compassed me about;' I shall not see the land that floweth with milk and honey. And with that a great darkness and horror fell upon Christian, so that he could not see before him. Also here he in a great measure lost his senses, so that he could neither remember nor orderly talk of any of those sweet refreshments that he had met with in the way of his pilgrimage. But all the words that he spoke still tended to discover that he had horror of mind, and heart fears that he should die in that river, and never obtain entrance in at the gate. Here also, as they who stood by perceived, he was much in the troublesome thoughts of the sins that he had committed both since and before he began to be a pilgrim. It was also observed that he was troubled with apparitions of hobgoblins and evil spirits; for ever and anon he would intimate so much by words.

Hopeful, therefore, here had much ado to keep his brother's head above water; yea, sometimes he would be quite gone down, and then, era a while, he would rise up again half dead. Hopeful also would endeavour to comfort him, saying, Brother, I see the gate, and men standing by to receive us; but Christian would answer, 'Tis you, 'tis you they wait for; you have been hopeful ever since I knew you. And so have you, said he to Christian. Ah brother, said he, surely if I were right he would now arise to help me: but for my sins he hath brought me into this snare, and hath left me. Then said Hopeful, My brother, . . . these troubles and distressess that you go through are no sign that God hath for-saken you; but are sent to try you, whether you will call to mind that which heretofore you have received of his goodness . . . .

Then I saw in my dream that Christian was in a muse awhile. To whom also Hopeful added these words, Be of good cheer, Jesus Christ maketh thee whole. And with that Christian break out with a loud voice, Oh, I see him again! And he tell me, 'When thou passest through the waters, I will be with thee; and through the rivers, they shall not overflow thee.' (Isaiah 43:2). Then they both took courage, and the enemy was after that as still as a stone until they were gone over. Christian, therefore, presently found ground to stand upon, and so it followed that the rest of the ground was but shallow: thus they got over.

Now, upon the bank of the river, on the other side, they saw the two Shining Men again, who were waited for them. Wherefore, being come out of the river, they saluted them, saying, 'We are ministering spirits, sent forth to minister to those that shall be heirs of salvation.' Thus they went towards the gate.

Now you must note, that the City stood upon a mighty hill; but the pilgrims went up that hill with ease, because they had these two men to lead them up by the arm; they had likewise left their mortal garments behind them in the river; for though they went in with them, they came out without them. They therefore went up here with much agility and speed, though the foundation upon which the City was framed was higher than the clouds; they, therefore, went up through the regions of the air, sweetly talking as they went, being comforted because they safely got over the river, and had such glorious companions to attend them.

The talk that they had with the Shining Ones was about the glory of the place; who told them that the beauty and the glory of it was inexpressible .... You are going now, said they, to the paradise of God, wherein you shall see the tree of life, and eat of the never-fading fruits thereof: and when you come there you shall have white robes given you, and your walk and talk shall be every day with the King, even all the days of eternity. There you shall not see again such things as you saw when you were in the lower region upon the earth — to wit, sorrow, sickness, affliction, and death; 'for the former things are passed away.' (Isaiah 65:16, 17) .... In that place you must wear crowns of gold, and enjoy the perpetual sight and visions of the Holy One; for 'there you shall see him as he is.' (1 John 3:2). There, also, you shall serve him continually with praise, with shouting, with thanksgiving, whom you desired to serve in the world, though with much difficulty because of the infimity of your flesh. There your eyes shall be delighted with seeing and your ears with hearing the pleasant voice of the Mighty One.... When he shall come with sound of trumpet in the clouds, as upon the wings of the wind, you shall come with him; and when he shall sit upon the throne of judgement, you shall sit by him; yea, and when he shall pass sentence upon all the workers of iniquity, let them be angels or men, you, also, shall have a voice in that judgement, because they were his and your enemies. Also, when he shall again return to the City, you shall go too, with sound of trumpet, and be ever with him. (1 Thessalonians 4:13-17; Jude 14, 15; Daniel 7:9 10; 1 Corinthians 6:2, 3.)

Now, while they were thus drawing towards the gate, behold a company of the heavenly host came out to meet them; to whom it was said by the other two Shining Ones, These are the men that have loved our Lord when they were in the world, and that have forsaken all for his holy name; and he hath sent us to fetch them, and we have brought them thus far on their desired journey, that they may go in and look their Redeemer in the face with joy. Then the heavenly host gave a great shout, saying, 'Blessed are they that are called to the marriage supper of the Lamb.' (Revelation 19:9.) They came out, also, at this time to meet them several of the King's trumpeters, clothed in white and shining raiment, who, with melodious voices, made even the heavens to echo with their sound. These trumpeters saluted Christian and his fellow with ten thousand welcomes from the world; and this they did with shouting and sound of trumpets.

This done, they compassed them round on every side ... continually sounding as they went, with melodious noise .... And now were these two men, as it were, in heaven, before they came at it, being swallowed up with the sight of angels, and with hearing their melodious notes. Here, also, they had the City itself in view; and thought they heard all the bells therein to ring, to welcome them thereto. But, above all, the warm and joyful thoughts that they had about their own dwelling there, with such company, and that for ever and ever; oh! by what tongue or pen can their glorious joy be expressed! Thus they came up to the gate.

Now, when they were come up to the gate, there was written over it, in letters of gold, 'BLESSED ARE THEY THAT DO HIS COMMANDMENTS, THAT THEY MAY HAVE RIGHT TO THE TREE OF LIFE, AND MAY ENTER IN THROUGH THE GATES INTO THE CITY.' (Revelation 22:14.)

Then I saw in my dreams that the Shining Men bid them call at the gate: the which when they did, some from above, looked over the gate ... to whom it was said, These pilgrims are come from the City of Destruction, for the love that they bare to the King of this place . . . . The King then commanded to open gate, 'that the righteous nation that keepeth the truth may enter in'. (Isaiah 26:2.)

Now I saw in my dream that these two men went in at the gate; and, lo! as they entered, they were transfigured; and they had raiment put on that shone like gold . . . . Then I heard in my dream, that the bells in the City rang again for joy, and that it was said unto them, 'ENTER YE INTO THE JOY OF OUR LORD.'

I also heard the men themselves sing with a loud voice, saying — 'BLESSING, AND HONOUR, AND GLORY, AND POWER, BE UNTO HIM THAT SITTETH UPON THE THRONE, AND UNTO THE LAMB, FOR EVER AND EVER.' (Revelation 5:13.)

Selections from

Pilgrim's Progress, Part Two

Christiana Begins Her Pilgrimage

Sometime since, to tell you my dream that I had of
Christian the Pilgrim ... was pleasant to me and
profitable to you. I told you then, also, what I saw
concerning his wife and children, and how unwilling
they were to go with him on pilgrimage ....

Now, it hath so happened, through the multiplicity
of business, that I have been much hindered and kept
back, from my wonted travels in those parts where he
went, and so could not, until now, obtain an
opportunity to make further inquiry after those whom
he left behind, that I might give you an account of
them. But having had some concerns that way of late, I
went down again thitherward. Now, having taken up
my lodgings in a wood about a mile off the place, as I
slept I dreamed again.

And, as I was in my dream, behold, an aged
gentleman came by the where I lay .... Sir, said, I, what
town is it there below, that lieth on the left hand of our
way?

Then said Mr. Sagacity (for that was his name), It is
the City of Destruction ....

I thought that was the city, quoth I; I went once
myself through that town .... Pray, did you ever hear

what happened to a man, some time ago, of this town (whose name was Christian), that went on a pilgrimage up towards the higher regions?

Sagacity: Hear of him! Ay, and I also heard of the molestations, troubles, wars, captivities, cries, groans, frights, and fears that he met with and had in his journey ....

But pray, sir, while it is fresh in my mind, do you hear anything of his wife and children?

Sagacity: Who? Christiana and her sons? They are like to do as well as Christian did himself; for though they all played the fool at first, and would by no means be persuaded by either the tears or entreaties of Christian, yet second thoughts have wrought wonderfully with them: so they have packed up, and are also gone after him.

Better and better, quoth I; but, what! wife and children and all?

Sagacity: It is true: I can give you an account of the matter, for I was upon the spot at the instant, and was thoroughly acquainted with the whole affair ....

They are gone on pilgrimage, both the good woman and her four boys. And seeing we are, as I perceive, going some considerable way together, I will give you an account of the whole matter.

This Christiana..., after her husband was gone over the river, and she could hear of him no more, began to have thoughts working in her mind .... Christiana did also begin to consider with herself, whether her unbecoming behaviour towards her husband was not one cause that she saw him no more .... Yea, there was not anything that Christian either said to her, or did before her, all the while that his burden did hang on his back, but it returned upon her like a flash of lightning,

51

and rent the caul of her heart in sunder; especially that bitter outcry of his, 'What shall I do to be saved?' did ring in her ears most dolefully.

Then said she to her children, Sons, we are all undone. I have sinned away your father, and he is gone: he would have had us with him, but I would not go myself: I also have hindered you of life.

With that the boys fell all into tears, and cried out to go after their father. Oh! said Christiana, that it had been but our lot to go with him, then had it fared well with us, beyond what it is like to do now . . . .

The next night Christiana had a dream: and, behold, she saw as if a broad parchment was open before her, in which was recorded the sum of her ways; and the times, as she thought, looked very black upon her. Then she cried out aloud in her sleep, 'Lord have mercy upon me a sinner!'; and the little children heard her.

After this, she thought she saw two very ill-favoured ones standing by her bedside, and saying, What shall we do with this woman? for she cries out for mercy, waking and sleeping. If she be suffered to go on as she begins, we shall lose her, as we have lost her husband. Wherefore we must, by one way or other, seek to take her off from the thoughts of what shall be hereafter, else all the world cannot help but she will become a pilgrim.

Now she woke in a great sweat; also a trembling was upon her; but after a while she fell to sleeping again. And then she thought she saw Christian her husband . . . before One that sat upon the throne, with a rainbow about his head. She saw, also, as if he bowed his head with his face to the paved work that was under the Prince's feet, saying, I heartily thank my Lord and King for bringing me into this place. Then shouted a company of them that stood round about, and harped with their harps . . . .

Next morning, when she was up, had prayed to God and talked with her children a while, one knocked hard at the door; to whom she spake, saying, If thou comest in God's name, come in. So he said, Amen, and opened the door, and saluted her with, Peace be to this house. To which, when he had done, he said, Christiana, knowest thou wherefore I am come? Then she blushed and trembled; also her heart began to wax warm with desires to know from whence he came, and what was his errand to her. So he said unto her, My name is Secret . . . . There is a report that thou art aware of the evil thou hast formerly done to thy husband, in hardening of thy heart against his way, and in keeping of these babes in their ignorance. Christiana, the Merciful One hath sent me to tell thee, that he is a God ready to forgive, and that he taketh delight to multiply the pardon of offences. He also would have thee to know, that he inviteth thee to come into his presence, to his table, that he will feed thee with the fat of his house, and with the heritage of Jacob thy father . . . .

This visitor proceeded, and said, Christiana, here is also a letter for thee, which I have brought to thee from thy husband's King. She took it, and opened it . . . . It was written in letters of gold. The contents of the letter were these: That the King would have her to do as Christian, her husband, for that was the way to come to his city, and to dwell in his presence with joy for ever. At this the good woman was quite overcome; so she cried out to her visitor, Sir, will you carry me and my children with you, that we also may go and worship the King?

Then said the visitor, Christiana, the bitter is before the sweet. Thou must through troubles, as did he that went before thee, enter this Celestial City. Wherefore, I advise thee to do as did Christian, thy husband; go to the Wicket-gate yonder over the plain, for that stands at the head of the way up which you must go, and I wish thee all good speed. Also, I advise that you put this letter in thy bosom . . . . This thou must deliver in at the farther gate . . . .

So Christiana called her sons together, and began thus to address herself unto them: . . . Come, my children, let us pack up, and be gone to the gate that leads to the Celestial country, that we may see your father, and be with him and his companions in peace . . . .

From The Wicket-Gate

Wherefore, methought I saw Christiana, and Mercy, and the boys, go all of them up to the gate; to which when they were come, they betook themselves to a short debate about how they must manage their calling at the gate, and what should be said unto him that did open to them: so it was concluded, since Christiana was the eldest, that she should knock for entrance, and that she should speak to him that did open, for the rest. So Christiana began to knock, and, as her poor husband did, she knocked and knocked again. But, instead of any that answered, they all thought that they heard as if a dog came barking upon them; a dog, and a great one too: and this made the women and children afraid. Nor durst they for a while to knock any more, for fear the mastiff should fly upon them. Now, therefore, they were greatly tumbled up and down in their minds, and knew not what to do: knock they durst not, for fear of the dog; go back they durst not, for fear the keeper of the gate should espy them as they so went, and should be offended with them: at last they thought of knocking again, and knocked more vehemently than they did at first. Then said the keeper of the gate, Who is there? So the dog left off to bark, and he opened unto them.

Then Christiana made low obeisance, and said ..., We are from whence Christian did come, and upon the same errand as he, to wit, to be, if it shall please you, graciously admitted by this gate, into the way that leads to the Celestial City .... With that the keeper of the gate did marvel, saying, What! is she now become a pilgrim, that but a while ago abhorred that life? Then she bowed her head, and said, Yes; amd so are these, my sweet babes, also.

Then he took her by the hand and led her in, and said, also, Suffer the little children to come unto me ....

So I saw in my dream that they walked on their way .... Now there was, on the other side of the wall that fenced in the way up which Christiana and her companions were to go, a garden, and that garden belonged to him whose was that barking dog, of whom mention was made before. And some of the fruit trees that they grew in that garden shot their branches over the wall; and, being mellow, that they found them did gather them up, and eat of them to their hurt. So Christiana's boys (as boys are apt to do) being pleased with the trees, and with the fruit that hung thereon, did pluck them, and began to eat. Their mother did also chide them for so doing, but still the boys went on.

Well, said she, my sons, you transgress, for that fruit is none of ours: but she did not know that it belonged to the enemy. I'll warrant you, if she had, she would have been ready to die for fear. But that passed, and they went on their way. Now, by that they were gone about two bow-shots from the place that led them into the way, they espied two very ill-favoured ones coming down apace to meet them. With that, Christiana, and Mercy her friend, covered themselves with their veils, and so kept on their journey; the children, also, went on before: so at last they met together. Then they that came down to meet them came just up to the women, as if they would embrace them: but Christiana said, Stand back, or go peacably as you should. Yet these two, as men that are deaf, regarded not Christiana's words, but began to lay hands upon them: at that Christiana, waxing very wroth spurned at them with her feet. Mercy, also, as well as she could, did what she could to shift them. Christiana again said to them, Stand back, and be gone; for we have no money to lose, being pilgrims, as you see, and such, too, as live upon the charity of our friends.

Then said one of the two men, We make no assault upon you for money, but are come out to tell you, that if you will but grant one small request which we shall ask, we will make women of you forever.

Now Christiana, imagining what they should mean, made answer again, We will neither hear, nor regard, nor yield to what you shall ask. We are in haste, and cannot stay; our business is a business of life and death. So again she and her companion made a fresh assay to go past them; but they letted them in their way.

And they said, We intend no hurt to your lives; 'tis another thing we would have.

Ay, quoth Christiana, you would have us body and soul, for I know tis for that you are come; but we will die rather upon the spot, than to suffer ourselves to be brought into such snares as shall hazard our wellbeing hereafter. And with that they both shrieked out and cried, Murder! murder! . . . .

Now, they being, as I said, not far from the gate in at which they came, their voice was heard from whence they were, thither; wherefore, some of the house came out, and knowing that it was Christiana's tongue, they made haste to her relief. But by that they were got within sight of them, the women were in a very great scuffle; the children, also, stood crying by. Then did he that came in for their relief call out to the roughians, saying, What is that thing you do? Would you make my Lord's people to transgress? He also attempted to take them; but they did make their escape over the wall into the garden of the man to whom the great dog belonged; so the dog became their protector. This Reliever then came up to the women, and asked them how they did. So they answered, We think thy Prince, pretty well, only we have been somewhat affrighted; we thank thee also, for that thou camest in to our help, otherwise we had been overcome . . . .

The Interpreter than called for a man-servant of his, one Great-heart, and bid him take sword, and helmet, and shield; and take these, my daughters, said he, conduct them to the house called Beautiful, at which place they will rest next. So he took his weapons and went with them; and the Interpreter said, God speed
. . . .

Now I saw in my dream that they went on, and Great-heart before them. So they went and came to the place where Christian's burden fell off his back, and tumbled into the sepulchre. Here, then, they made a pause; and here, also, they blessed God. Now, said Christiana, it comes to my mind what was said to us at the gate — to wit, that we should have pardon by word and deed: by word, that is, by the promise; by deed, to wit, in the way it was obtained. What the promise is, of that I know something; but what it is to have pardon by deed, or in the way that it was obtained, Mr. Great-heart, I suppose you know; wherefore, if you please, let us hear you discourse thereof.

Great-heart: Pardon by the deed done, is pardon obtained by someone, for another that hath need thereof: not by the person pardoned, but in the way, saith another, in which I have obtained it. So, then, to speak to the question more at large, the pardon that you, and Mercy, and these boys have attained, was obtained by another; to wit, by him that let you in at the gate: and he hath obtained by another; to wit, by him that let you in at the gate: and he hath obtained it in this double way; he has performed a righteousness to cover you, and spilt his blood to wash you in .... Wherefore he saith, 'As by one man's disobedience many were made sinners; so by the obedience of one shall many be made righteous.' (Romans 5:19.) ....

Christiana: Though my heart was lightsome and joyous before, yet it is ten times more lightsome and joyous now ....

So they went on, till they came within sight of the lions. Now Mr. Great-heart was a strong man, so he was not afraid of the lions; but yet, when they were come up to the place where the lions were, the boys that went before were now glad to cringe behind, for they were afraid of the lions; so they stepped back, and went behind. At this their guide smiled, and said, How now, my boys; do you love to go before when no danger doth approach, and love to come behind so soon as the lions appear?

Now as they went on, Mr. Great-heart drew his sword, with an intent to make a way for the pilgrims in spite of the lions. Then there appeared one that, it seems, had taken upon him to back the lions; and he said to the pilgrims' guide, What is the cause of your coming hither? Now, the name of that man was Grim, or Bloody-man because of his slaying of pilgrims; and he was of the race of the giants.

Then said the pilgrims' guide, These women and children are going on pilgrimage; and this is the way they must go; and go it they shall, in spite of thee and the lions . . . .

Then said he that attempted to back the lions, Will you slay me upon my own ground?

Great-heart: It is the King's highway that we are in, and in this way it is that thou hast placed the lions; but these women and these children, though weak, shall hold on their way in spite of thy lions. And with that he gave him a downright blow, and brought him upon his knees. With this blow, also, he broke his helmet, and with the next he cut off an arm. Then did the giant roar so hideously, that his voice frightened the women; and yet they were glad to see him lie sprawling upon the ground. Now the lions were chained, and so of themselves could do nothing. Wherefore, when old Grim, that intended to back them, was dead, Mr. Great-heart said to the pilgrims, Come now, and follow me, and no hurt shall happen to you from the lions . . . .

The End Of Giant Despair

Now they went. And when they were come to By-path Meadow, to the stile over which Christian went with his fellow Hopeful, when they were taken by Giant Despair and put into Doubting Castle, they sat down and consulted what was best to be done — to wit, now that they were so strong, and had got such a man as Mr. Great-heart for their conductor, whether they had not best to make an attempt upon the giant, demolish his castle, and if there were any pilgrims in it, to set them at liberty before they went any farther. So one said one thing, and another said the contrary. One questioned if it were lawful to go upon unconsecrated ground: and other said they might, provided their end was good; but Mr. Great-heart said, Though that assertion offered last cannot be universally true, yet I have a commandment to resist sin, to overcome evil, to fight the good fight of faith; and, I pray, with whom should I fight this good fight, if not with Giant Despair? I will, therefore, attempt the taking away of his life and the demolishing of Doubting Castle. Then said he, Who will go with me? Then said old Honest, I will. And so will we too, said Christiana's four sons, Matthew, Samuel, Joseph and James; for they were young men and strong . . . .

So Mr. Great-heart, old Honest, and the four young men, went to go up to Doubting Castle, to look for Giant Despair. When they came to the castle gate, they knocked for entrance with an unusual noise. At that the old giant came to the gate, and Diffidence his wife follows. Then said he, Who and what is he that is so hardy as after this manner to molest the Giant Despair?

Mr. Great-heart replied, It is I, Great-heart, one of the King of the Celestial Country's conductors of pilgrims to their place; and I demand of thee that thou open thy gates for my entrance; prepare thyself also to fight, for I am come to take away thy head, and to demolish Doubting Castle.

Now Giant Despair, because he was a giant, thought no man could overcome him; and again thought he, Since heretofore I have made a conquest of angels, shall Great-heart make me afraid? So he harnessed himself, and went out. He had a cap of steel upon his head, a breastplate of fire girded to him, and he came out in iron shoes, and with a great club in his hand. Then the six men made up to him, and beset him behind and before; also, when Diffidence, the giantess, came up to help him, old Mr. Honest cut her down with one blow. Then they fought for their lives, and Giant Despair was brought down to the ground, but was very loth to die. He struggled hard, and had, as they say, as many lives as a cat; but Great-heart was his death, for he left him not till he had severed his head from his shoulders. Then they fell to demolishing Doubting Castle, and that, you know, might with ease be done, since Giant Despair was dead. They were seven days in destroying of that; and in it of pilgrims they found one Mr. Despondency, almost starved to death, and one Much-afraid, his daughter: these two they saved alive. But it would have made you wonder to have seen the dead bodies that lay here and there in the castle yard, and how full of dead men's bones the dungeon was . . . .

Valiant - For - Truth

Then they went on; . . . there stood a man with a sword drawn and his face all over with blood. Then said Mr. Great-heart, Who art thou? The man made answer, saying, I am one whose name is Valiant-for-truth. I am a pilgrim, and I am going to the Celestial City. Now, as I was in my way, there were three men that did beset me, and propounded unto me these three things: 1. Whether I would become one of them. 2. Or go back from whence I came. 3. Or die upon the place. To the first I answered, I had been a true man for a long season, and therefore it could not be expected that I should now cast in my lot with thieves. Then they demanded what I should say to the second. So I told them, the place from whence I came, had I not found incommodity there, I had not forsaken it at all; but finding it altogether unsuitable to me, and very unprofitable for me, I forsook it for this way. Then they asked me what I said to the third. And I told them, my life cost far more dear that I should lightly give it away . . . . Then these three — to wit, Wild-head, Inconsiderate, and Pragmatic drew upon me and I also drew upon them. So we fell to it, one against three, for the space of above three hours. They have left upon me, as you see, some of the marks of their valour, and have also carried away with them some of mine . . . .

Great-heart: But here was great odds, three against one.

Valiant-for-truth: 'Tis true; but little or more are nothing to him that hath the truth on his side: 'Though an host should encamp against me my heart shall not fear . . .'.

Great-heart: Why did you not cry out? that some might have come for your succour?

Valiant-for-truth: So I did to my King, who I knew would hear me and afford invisible help, and that was sufficient for me . . . .

Great-heart: Thou hast done well; thou hast resisted unto blood, striving against sin. Thou shalt abide by us; come in and go out with us, for we are thy companions. Then they took him and washed his wounds, and gave him of what they had to refresh him: and so they went together . . . .

Great-heart: This was your victory, even your faith.

Valiant-for-truth: It was so. I believed, and therefore came out, got into the way, fought all that set themselves against me, and, by believing, am come to this place.

> Who would true valour see,
> Let him come hither;
> One here will constant be,
> Come wind, come weather;
> There's no discouragement
> Shall make him once relent
> His first avowed intent
> To be a pilgrim.
>
> Whoso beset him round
> With dismal stories
> Do but themselves confound;
> His strength the more is.
> No lion can him fright,
> He'll with a giant fight,
> But he will have a right
> To be a pilgrim.

Hobgoblin nor foul fiend
Can daunt his spirit;
He knows he at the end
Shall life inherit.
Then fancies fly away,
He'll not fear what men say;
He'll labour night and day
To be a pilgrim.

By this time they were got to the Enchanted Ground, where the air naturally tended to make one drowsy.

And that place was all grown over with briars and thorns, excepting here and there, where was an exchanted arbour, upon which, if a man sits, or in which, if a man sleeps, it is a question, some say, whether ever he shall rise or wake again in this world. Over this forest, therefore, they went, both one and another, and Mr. Great-heart went before, for that he was the guide; and Mr. Valiant-for-truth came behind, being rearguard, for fear lest peradventure some fiend or dragon, or giant, or thief should fall upon their rear, and so do mischief . . . .

I saw them in my dream, that they went on in this their solitary ground, till they came to a place at which a man is apt to lose his way. Now, though when it was light, their guide could well enough tell how to miss those ways that led wrong, yet in the dark he was put to a stand, But he had in his pocket a map of all ways leading to or from the Celestial City; wherefore he struck a light, and takes a view of his book or map, which bids him to be careful in that place to turn to the right hand. And had he not been careful here to look in his map, they had, in all probability, been smothered in the mud . . . .

The Land Of Beulah

After this I beheld until they were come into the land of Beulah, where the sun shineth night and day. Here, because they were weary, they betook themselves a while to rest. And because this country was common for pilgrims, and because the orchards and vineyards that were there belonged to the King of Celestial country, therefore they were licensed to make bold with any of his things. But a little while soon refreshed them here; for the bells did so ring, and the trumpets continually sound so melodiously, that they could not sleep, and yet they received as much refreshing as if they had slept their sleep ever so soundly . . . .

Now, while they lay here and waited for the good hour, there was a noise in the town that there was a post come from the Celestial City, with a matter of great importance to one Christiana, the wife of Christian the pilgrim. So inquiry was made for her, and the house was found out where she was. So the post presented her with a letter. The contents were, Hail, good woman; I bring thee tidings that the Master calleth for thee, and expects that thou shouldst stand in his presence, in clothes of immortality, within these ten days . . . .

When Christiana saw that her time was come, and that she was the first of this company that was to go over, she called for Mr. Great-heart her guide, and told him how matters were . . . . Then she called for her children, and gave them her blessing; and told them that she had read with comfort the mark that was set in their foreheads, and was glad to see them with her there, and that they had kept their garments so white . . . .

Then she called for old Mr. Honest .... Said he, I wish you a fair day when you set out for Mount Zion; and shall be glad to see that you go over the river dry shod. But she answered, Come wet, come dry, I long to be gone ....

Now the day drew on that Christiana must be gone. So the road was full of people to see her take her journey. But, behold, all the banks beyond the river were full of horses and chariots, which were come down from above to accompany her to the city gate. So she came forth and entered the river, with a beckon of farewell to those that followed her. The last words that she was heard to say were, I come, Lord, to be with thee, and bless thee!

... And for Christiana's children — the four boys that Christiana brought, with their wives and children — I did not stay where I was till they were gone over. Also, since I came away, I heard one say that they were yet alive, and so would be, for the increase of the Church in that place where they were, for a time.

Selections from

The Jerusalem Sinner Saved;
or Good News for the Vilest of Men

Beginning At Jerusalem

This clause is in special mentioned by Luke, who saith, that as Christ would have the doctrine of repentance and remission of sins preached in his name among all nations, so he would have the people of Jerusalem to have the first proffer thereof . . . .

Jerusalem . . . . was the place and seat of God's worship, but now decayed, degenerated, apostacised . . . . Jerusalem was therefore now greatly backslidden, and become the place where truth and true religion were much defaced.

It was also now become the very sink of sin and seat of hypocrisy, and gulf where true religion was drowned . . . . In a word, Jerusalem was now become the shambles, the very slaughter-shop for saints. This was the place wherein the prophets, Christ, and his people, were most horribly persecuted and murdered. Yea, so hardened at this time was this Jerusalem in her sins, that she feared not to commit the biggest and to bind herself, by wish, under the guilt and damning evil of it; saying, when she had murdered the Son of God, 'His blood be upon us, and on our children.' . . . . What world, what people, what nation, for sin and

transgression, could or can be compared to Jerusalem?
. . .

Whatever, therefore, their relation was to Abraham, Isaac, or Jacob — however they formerly had been the people among whom God had placed his name and worship, they were now degenerated from God, more than the nations were from their idols, and were become guilty of the highest sins which the people of the world were capable of committing. Nay, none can be capable of committing of such pardonable sins as they committed against their God, when they slew his Son, and persecuted his name and Word.

From these words, therefore, thus explained, we gain this observation: -

That Jesus Christ would have mercy offered in the first place, to the biggest sinners.

. . . One would a-thought, since the Jerusalem sinners were the worst and greatest sinners, Christ's greatest enemies, and those that not only despised his person, doctrine, and miracles, but that, a little before, had had their hands up to the elbows in his heart's blood, that he should rather have said, Go into all the world, and preach repentance and remission of sins among all nations; and, *after* that, offer the same to Jerusalem; yea, it had been infinitely grace if he had said so. But what grace in this, or what name shall we give it, when he commands that this repentance and remission of sins, which is designed to be preached in all nations, should first be offered to Jerusalem; in the first place to the worst of sinners! . . .

Nor did the apostles overlook this clause when their Lord was gone into heaven; . . . the first sermon which they preached after the ascension of Christ, it was preached to the very worst of these Jerusalem sinners, even to those that were the murderers of Jesus Christ (Act 2:29) . . . . Yea, the next sermon, and the next, and also the next to that, was preached to the self-same murderers, to the end they might be saved. (Acts 3:14, 16; 4:10, 11; 5:30; 7:52.)

. . . So far off was Peter from making an objection against one of them, that, by a particular clause in his exhortation, he endeavours, that not one of them may escape the salvation offered. 'Repent,' saith he, 'and be baptized every one of you.' . . .

Objector: 'But I was one of them that plotted to take away his life. May I be saved by him?'

Peter: Every one of you.

Objector: 'But I was one of them that bear false witness against him. Is there grace for me?'

Peter: For every one of you.

Objector: 'But I was one of them that cried out, Crucify him, crucify him; and desired that Barabbas, the murderer might live, rather than him. What will become of me, think you?'

Peter; I am to preach repentance and remission of sins to every one of you.

Objector: 'But I was one of them that did spit in his face when he stood before his accusers. I also was one that mocked him, when in anguish he hanged bleeding on the tree. Is there room for me?'

Peter: For every one of you.

Objector: 'But I was one of them that, in his extremity, said, Give him gall and vinegar to drink. Why may not I expect the same when anguish and guilt is upon me?'

Peter: Repent of these your wickednesses, and here

is remission of sins for every one of you.

Objector: 'But I railed on him, I reviled him, I hated him, I rejoiced to see him mocked at by others. Can there be hopes for me?'

Peter: There is, for every one of you . . . .

Christ would not take their first rejection for a denial, nor their second repulse for a denial; but he will have grace offered once, and twice, and thrice, to these Jerusalem sinners. Is not this amazing grace? . . . Nor was their preaching unsuccessful among these people . . . three thousand of them closed with him at the first; and, afterwards, two thousand and more; for now they were in number about five thousand; whereas, before sermons were preached to these murderers, the number of the disciples was not above 'a hundred and twenty'.

Also among those that thus flocked to him for mercy, there was a 'great company of the priests'. Now the priests were they that were the greatest of these biggest sinners; they were the ringleaders, they were the inventors and ringleaders in the mischief. It was they that set the people against the Lord Jesus, and were the cause why the uproar increased, until Pilate had given sentence upon him . . . . And yet, behold the priests, yea, a great company of the priests, became obedient to the faith.

Oh, the greatness of the grace of Christ, that he should be thus in love with the souls of Jerusalem sinners!

Why This Amazing Grace?

Christ Jesus, as you may perceive, has put himself under the term of a physician, a doctor for curing of diseases; and you know that applause and fame are things that physicians much desire. That is it that helps them to patients; and that, also, that will help their patients to commit themselves to their skill for cure, with the more confidence and repose of spirit . . . . Physicians get neither name nor fame by pricking of wheals, or picking out thistles, or by laying of plasters to the scratch of a pin; every old woman can do this. But if they would have a name and a fame, if they will have it quickly, they must, as I said, do some great and desperate cures . . . .

Why, Christ Jesus forgiveth sins for a name, and so begets for himself a good report in the hearts of the children of men. And, therefore, in reason he must be willing, as also, he did command, that his mercy should be offered first to the biggest sinner. I will forgive their sins, iniquities, and transgressions, says he, 'And it shall be to me a name of joy, a praise and an honour, before all nations of the earth.' . . . .

Christ, as I said, has put himself under the term of a physician; consequently he desireth that his fame, as to the salvation of sinners, may spread abroad, that the world may see what he can do. And to this end, has not only commanded that the biggest sinners should have the first offer of his mercy, but has, as physicians do, put out his bills, and published his doings, that things may be read and talked of. Yea, he has, moreover, in these, his blessed bills, the holy Scriptures I mean, inserted the very names of persons, the places of their abode, and the great cures that, by the means of his salvation, he was wrought upon them to this very end. Here is, *Item*, such a one, by my grace and redeeming blood, was made a monument of everlasting life; and such a one, by my perfect obedience, became an heir of glory. And then he produceth their name. *Item*, I saved Lot from guilt and damnation that he had procured for himself by his incest. *Item*, I saved David from the vengeance that belonged to him for committing of adultery and murder. Here is, also, Solomon, Manasseh, Peter, Magdalene, and many others, made mention of in this book. Yea, here are their names, their sins, and their salvations recorded together, that you may read and know what a Saviour he is, and do him honour in the world. For why are these things thus recorded, but to show to sinners what he can do, to the praise and glory of his grace? And it is observable as I said before, we have but very little of the salvation of little sinners mentioned in God's book, because that would not have answered the design, to wit, to bring glory and fame to the name of the Son of God . . . .

When Christ was crucified and hanged up between the earth and heavens, there were two thieves crucified with him, and behold, he lays hold of one of them, and will have him away with him to glory. Was not this a strange act, and a display of unthought-of grace? Where there none but thieves there, or were the rest of that company out of his reach? Could he not, think you, have stooped from the cross to the ground, and have laid hold on some honester man, if he would? Yes, doubtless. Oh! but then he would not have displayed his grace, nor so have pursued his own designs, namely, to get to himself of praise and a name; but must confess, that the Son of God is full of grace;

for a proof of the riches thereof, he left behind him, when, upon the cross, he took the thief away with him to glory. Nor can this one act of his be buried; it will be talked of, to the end of the world, to his praise . . . .

For the physician, by curing the most desperate at the first, doth not only get himself a name, but begets encouragement in the minds of other diseased folk to come to him for help. Hence you read of our Lord that after, through his tender mercy, he did cure many of great diseases, his fame was spread abroad . . . . He proffers his grace, in the first place, to the biggest sinners, that others may take heart to come to him to be saved . . . . 'God,' saith Paul, 'who is rich in mercy, for his great love wherewith he loved us, even when we were dead in sins, hath quickened us together with Christ (by grace ye are saved); and hath raised us up together, and made us sit together in heavenly places in Christ Jesus.' But why did he do this? 'That in the ages to come he might show the exceeding riches of his grace in his kindness towards us through Christ Jesus.' (Ephesians 2: 4-7.) . . . .

But what was Paul himself? Why, he tells you himself; I am, says he, the chief of sinners. I was, says he, a blasphemer, a persecutor, an injurious person; but I obtained mercy. (1 Timothy 1:13, 14.) Ay, that is well for you, Paul; but what advantage have we thereby? Oh, very much, saith he; for, 'for this cause I obtained mercy, that in me first Jesus Christ might show forth all long-suffering, for a pattern to them which should hereafter believe on him to life everlasting' (verse 16) . . . .

The biggest sinners, they are Satan's colonels and captains, the leaders of his people, and they most stoutly make head against the Son of God. Wherefore, let these first be conquered, and his kingdom will be weak ....

I speak by experience. I was one of these ...; I infected all the youth of the town where I was born, with all manner of youthful vanities. The neighbours counted me so; my practise proved me so: wherefore, Christ Jesus took me first; and taking me first, the contagion was much allayed all the town over. When God made me sigh, they would hearken, and inquiringly say, What's the matter with John? They also gave their various opinions of me; but, as I said, sin cooled, and failed, as to his full career. When I went out to seek the bread of life, some of them would follow, and the rest be put into a muse at home. Yea, almost the town, at first, at times, would go out to hear at the place where I found good; yea, young and old for a while had some reformation on them, also some of them. perceiving that God had mercy upon me, came crying to him for mercy too ....

'Beginning at Jerusalem'. Our text says, that Jesus Christ bids preachers, in their preaching repentance and remission of sins, begin first at Jerusalem; thereby declaring most truly the infinite largeness of the merciful heart of God and his Son, to the sinful children of men .... It declares, that there is sufficiency in his blood to save the biggest sinners ....

Were therefore the tempted but aware, he might say, 'Ay, Satan, I am a sinner of the biggest size, and therefore have most need of Jesus Christ; yea, because I am such a wretch, therefore Jesus Christ calls me; yea, he calls me first; the first proffer of the Gospel is to be made to the Jerusalem sinner; I am he, wherefore stand back, Satan; make a lane, my right is first to come to Jesus Christ.'

Selections from

Come and Welcome to Jesus Christ

'Him that cometh to me I will in no wise cast out.' John 6:37.

There is many a sad wretch given by the Father to Jesus Christ; but not one of them all is despised or slighted by him. It is said of those that the Father hath given to Christ that they have done worse than the heathen; that they were murderers, thieves, drunkards, unclean persons, and whatnot; but he has received them, washed them, and saved them . . . .

Let him be as red as blood, let him be as red as crimson. Some men are blood-red sinners, crimson-sinners, sinners of a double dye, dipped and dipped again, before they come to Jesus Christ. Art thou that readest these lines such an one? Speak out, man! Art thou such an one? and art thou not coming to Jesus Christ for the mercy of justification, that thou mightest be made white in his blood, and be covered with his righteousness? Fear not; for as much as this thy coming betokeneth that thou art of the number of them that the Father hath given to Christ; for he will in no wise cast thee out. 'Come now,' saith Christ, 'and let us reason together; though your sins be as scarlet they shall be as white as snow; though they be red like crimson, they shall be as wool.' (Isaiah 1:18.) . . . .

'In no wise,' that is, for no sin . . . . Coming sinner, what promise thou findest in the word of Christ, strain it whither thou canst, so thou dost not corrupt it, and his blood and merits will answer all; what the word sayeth, or any true consequence that is drawn therefrom, that we may boldly venture upon. As here in the text he saith, 'And him that cometh,' indefinitely, without the least intimation of the rejection of any, though never so great, if he be a coming sinner. Take it then for granted, that thou, whoever thou art, if coming, art intended in these words; neither shall it injure Christ at all, if ... thou shalt catch him at his word ....

'And him that cometh.' There are two sorts of sinners that are coming to Jesus Christ. First, him that hath never, while of late, hath all began to come. Second, him that came formerly, and after that went back; but hath since bethought himself, and is now coming again. Both these sorts of sinners are intended by him in the text, as is evident; because both are now the coming sinners.

First. For the first of these: the sinner that hath never, while of late, began to come, his way is more easy; I do not say, more plain and open to come to Christ than is the other — those last not having the clog of a guilty conscience, for the sin of backsliding. But all the encouragement of the Gospel, and with what invitations are therein contained to coming sinners, are as free and as open to the one as to the other; so that they may with the same freedom and liberty, as from the Word, both alike claim interest in the promise. 'And let him that is athirst come.' (Revelation 22:17.)

Second. That the backslider is intended is evident, for that he is sent to by name, 'Go, tell his disciples and Peter,' (Mark 16:7.) But Peter was a godly man. True,

76

but he was also a backslider, yea, desperate backslider; he had denied his Master once, twice, thrice, cursing and swearing that he knew him not ....

Again, when David had backslidden, and had committed adultery and murder in his backsliding, he must be sent to by name: 'And,' saith the text, 'the Lord sent Nathan unto David.' And he sent him to tell him, after he had brought him to unfeigned acknowledgement, 'The Lord hath also put away, or forgiven, thy sins.' (II Samuel 12:1, 13.)

This man also was far gone; he took a man's wife, and killed her husband, and endeavoured to cover all with wicked dissimulation ....

But I am a great sinner, sayest thou.

'I will in no wise cast out' says Christ.

But I am an old sinner, sayest thou.

'I will in no wise cast out,' says Christ.

But I am a hard-hearted sinner, sayest thou.

'I will in no wise cast out,' says Christ.

But I am a backsliding sinner, sayest thou.

'I will in no wise cast out,' says Christ.

But I have served Satan all my days, sayest thou.

'I will in no wise cast, out,' says Christ.

But I have sinned against light, sayest thou.

'I will in no wise cast out,' says Christ.

But I have sinned against mercy, sayest thou.

'I will in no wise cast out,' says Christ.

But I have no good thing to bring with me, sayest thou.

'I will in no wise cast out,' says Christ.

Selections from

Mr. Bunyan's last sermon: preached August 19th, 1688, twelve days before his decease

'Which were born, not of blood, nor of the will of the flesh, nor of the will of man, but of God.' John 1:13.
A child, before it be born into the world, is in the dark dungeon of its mother's womb: so a child of God, before he be born again, is in the dark dungeon of sin, sees nothing of the kingdom of God; therefore it is called a new birth: the same soul has love one way in its carnal condition, another way when it is born again . . . .

A child, you know, is incident to cry as soon as it comes into the world; for if there be no noise, they say it is dead. You that are born of God and Christians, if you be no cryers, there is no spiritual life in you — if you be born of God, you are crying ones; as soon as he has raised you out of the dark dungeon of sin, you cannot but cry to God, What must I do to be saved? ....

It is not only natural for a child to cry, but it must crave the breast; it cannot live without the breast — therefore Peter makes it the true trial of a new-born babe: the new-born babe desives the sincere milk of the Word, that he may grow thereby . . . .

The child that is newly born, if it have not other comforts to keep it warm than it had in its mother's womb, it dies; it must have something got for its succour: so Christ had swaddling clothes prepared for him; so those that are born again, they must have some promise of Christ to keep them alive; those that are in a carnal state, they warm themselves with other things . . . . What fine things has Christ prepared to wrap all in that are born again! . . . . This is set out nothing in the world but the righteousness of Christ and the graces of the Spirit, without which a new-born babe cannot live, unless they have the righteousness of Christ . . . .

There us usually some similitude betwixt the father and the child. It may be the child looks like its father; so those that are born again, they have a new similitude — they have the image of Christ. (Galatians 4) Everyone that is born of God has something of the features of heaven upon him . . . .

Children, it is natural for them to depend upon their father for what they want; if they want a pair of shoes, they go and tell him; if they want bread, they go and tell him; so should the child of God do. Do you want spiritual bread? go tell God of it. Do you want strength of grace? ask it of God. Do you want strength against temptations? go and tell God of it. When the devil tempts you, run home and tell your heavenly Father — go pour out your complaints to God.